See! I am dancing!
On the rim of the world I am dancing!

– Ohlone Song

Nueva Cuenta

Freddy Gutierrez

Nomadic Press
2015

This book was made possible by a loving community of family and friends, old and new.

For author questions or to book a reading at your school, bookstore, or alternative establishment, please send an email to info@nomadicpress.org.

Published by Nomadic Press, 2926 Foothill Boulevard, Oakland, California, 94601
www.nomadicpress.org

First Edition
Second Printing

Printed in the United States

Library of Congress Cataloging-in-Publication Data
Gutierrez, Freddy, 1984 –
Nueva Cuenta/written by Freddy Gutierrez; illustrated by Arthur Johnstone and Livien Yin
p. cm.
Summary: Gutierrez's poems illuminate parallels between a personal sense of indigenized identity and the legacy of colonialism via the California Mission system and its impact on the local ecology.
[1. POETRY / American / Hispanic American. 2. POETRY / Subjects & Themes / Nature. 3. POETRY / Subjects & Themes / Places.] I. Title.

2015950567

ISBN: 978-0-9966172-2-2

The illustrations in this book were created using pen and marker on Canson paper.
The type was set in Garamond Premier Pro.
Printed and bound in the United States.
Typesetting and book design by J. K. Fowler.

The language from "Integral" is borrowed from *Impervious* by Jess Heaney (2013).

for the acorn and its people

CERO

El sueño
en el inframundo

like a fledgling
spirit   a wisp
in whisper

hidden beneath
the opaque huipil
of the mountain

waiting for the call
la lechusa
waiting for the white messenger

waiting for the bridge
coxamayotl
sobre el arcoíris pasan los niños
al vientre de sus mamas

INTEGRAL

Due to the arrival from the south of men and their cattle

The rains run down the tightly packed hills
into the tightly packed streams

Instead of sinking into the once-permeable soil

Carrying away the silt and flora, eroding the banks

UNO

El pensamiento
de un principio

Ce
o no sea
la verdad
que yo sea una de las plumas
entrado en el espacio de tu vientre
Coatlicue

sea
o no sea
la verdad
que yo era en la era de aquel entonces
que yo era un algo en la época del principio

a complex nature
of nature
you nutured the smallest of us

and I am
left-handed
a myth of turquoise

un rayo del cuento de nuestro origen
que reventó la desgracia de la de las campanas pintadas

and I paint a one stick poem
point with one finger toward sky
poke my heart with one

The creek used to be lined with plants

These plants cleaned the water, held the sediment and silt

They took and returned just the right amount

Ensuring stability

DOS

La unión, la dualidad
ometeotl

de los que vengo
double helixed
in utero in movement
ollin

I am two-spirits
I ome
de mi padre y de mi madre
I ome
yo dos por dos
encuentro cuatro manos que movieron
dos cuerpos con cuatro extremos
que me hicieron
hijo de dos
hijo de sol
hijo de oja

hijo de Anahuac
hijo de Borikén

deer grass sea thrift blue-eyed grass berkeley sedge
ceanothus mugwort

TRES

La reflexión
entre la casa del aprendizaje y el bosque

que yo sea un Nezahualcóyotl
cuando sea
as if I could be
such a noble beast
such a flowery man
a California lilac
wild with native roots
or orange
the state's blossom

west coast rising
to meet me in venison vision
a call to dream
coyote spirit dance
huarache prancing
third eye chasing deer movement
two hind paws de un perro perdido
prodigal hindsight
on oak land leaves
hungry and in famine

waiting for the fire
for my hardhead to burst piñón
and my heart to strike against mahogany obsidian
to learn to love stone
to grow sapling from ash
to stretch limbs
to photosynthesize the sun's movement
to bleed amber
to walk a path
leaf soft

california wild rose   yarrow   snowberry   alder   buckeye
coast live oak

CUATRO

El cuerpo
sobre la tierra

There are laws here
earthly governance
rules for the roaming of those who reach for the truth in

I learn to walk
I learn the lay of the land
I learn the land
I learn to work

learn that my hands can listen and speak
learn that feet can dance
                    rhythm for the wind
                    rhythm for the soil
                    rhythm for the waters
                    rhythm for the flame

GHOST BEADS

father Junípero Serra at my back
ghost beads across the chest

leafing through Ohlone feather skirts
searching for an origin
sifting through quaked beginnings

to see on what ground stands this new New World
dredging the old road of Alta California (the old New World)

PACIFIC COAST COLONIALS

to give the crown
such a valuable toehold in the frontier land
        el presidio

to give the church
such a precious ledge on God's earth
        la misión

and so militarism and religion
        the sword and the cross
        bared down against

                        the red wood and all its shelter
                        the tall grass and all its baskets
                        the hill clay and all its pottery
                        the obsidian and all its points
                        the oak and all its nourishment
                        the elder bush and all its music

OBJECTIVES FOR THE 21

CONVERT

conduct mass on days of high obligation

EDUCATE

establish settlements in areas of high concentrations

CIVILIZE

force their resettlement

*never stray from the coast

SHAPE SHIFTING

PASSIVE

refuse to learn the tongue
feign ignorance of command
perform slow and poor labor
practice infanticide and abortion
practice tradition in secret
                    to reverse the baptisms

FUGITIVISM

run away from the labor mills
                    be fit for the run
                    healthy for the hiding

OVERT

raid the stocks
sicken the padres
rise en masse

INTEGRAL

Due to design pavement and buildings are so impervious

The rains run down the tightly packed hills
into the tightly packed streams

Instead of sinking into the once-permeable soil

Carrying away the silt and flora, eroding the banks

OTHER AIMS

INTEGRATE

assimilate the neophytes into Spanish society

TRAIN

in ownership and management of the land

The creek used to be lined with plants

These plants cleaned the water, held the sediment and silt

They took and returned just the right amount

Ensuring stability

AMALGAMATIONS

Costeño people of the coast
Costano in the settler tongue
Costeño Costano cooked
          in a tongue twist of sea salt and acorn stew
and you, became ungainly, Costanoan

Or, as it fell upon your ears,
alone as Ohlone
          which might have been a name of place
          or
          orientation toward the house of the sun

Oh, Ohlone
          truly is this pleasing to your ear?
          truly does this fabrication suit you?
          suit the time
                    fiction for our human situation

Am I then of an Aztec?
Azteca
          (certainly awkward)
          or something more national?

And between the
points of nationhood
and Hidalgo's treaty
weren't we both
simply
Mexicanos?

deer grass sea thrift blue-eyed grass berkeley sedge ceanothus mugwort

IT WILL LIVE FOREVER

gather store process cook eat
gather store process cook eat
gather store process cook eat
gather store process cook eat
gather store process cook eat
gather store process cook eat
gather store process cook eat
gather store process cook eat
gather store process cook eat
gather store process cook eat
gather store process cook eat
gather store process cook eat
gather store process cook eat
gather store process cook eat
gather store process cook eat
gather store process cook eat
gather store process cook eat
gather store process cook eat
gather store process cook eat
gather store process cook eat
gather store process cook eat
gather store process cook eat
gather store process cook eat
gather store process cook eat
gather store process cook eat
gather store process cook eat
gather store process cook eat
gather store process cook eat

gather store process cook eat
gather store process cook eat
gather store process cook eat
gather store process cook eat
gather store process cook eat
gather store process cook eat
gather store process cook eat
gather store process cook eat
gather store process cook eat
gather store process cook eat
gather store process cook eat
gather store process cook eat
gather store process cook eat
gather store process cook eat
gather store process cook eat
gather store process cook eat
gather store process cook eat
gather store process cook eat
gather store process cook eat
gather store process cook eat
gather store process cook eat
gather store process cook eat
gather store process cook eat
gather store process cook eat
gather store process cook eat
gather store process cook eat
gather store process cook eat
gather store process cook eat

california wild rose   yarrow   snowberry   alder   buckeye
coast live oak

OF MIGHT

Might there have been poet warriors
mud-plume slingers
call 'em tar flickers;
if there ever existed such a thing,
may it exist now.

And then, might there be more of
          such colonial terrors
          such indigenous daughters
          such native sons
          such nonconforming children.
Tlacuilohs of the smoking tongue,
obsidian scribes and conch shell singers
colibri vatos de aquellos
hummingbird homegirls for the cause.

Might there be
more than so-called brown blight
on the gentro development
call 'em ruby throated shot callers
calling the jaguar thunder cats on the boulevard.

To recover.
To relearn.
To reclaim.

LONG COUNT

For thousands of years
a gathering of tules
a binding of bulrushes
a tuning of eagle bone
a knapping of flint
a weaving of tall grass
a managing of the forest
a stringing of abalone shell
a drilling of the fire
a flicking of turkey feathers
a building of the long house
a practicing of the earth ways

Freddy Gutierrez, *vato de aquellos*, MFA, accomplished writer, teaching artist, and cultural worker. Freddy inspires and nurtures writers to move from the page to the stage and the street. Freddy has taught with Youth Speaks, Chapter 510, and the Oakland Public Library. He facilitates writing and performance arts spaces with men and youth who are policed, imprisoned, and marginalized by the prison-industrial complex. Freddy has read and performed at cultural centers, universities, jails, and juvenile halls throughout Northern California. His poetry is a call for positive male socialization, immigrant rights, and against the criminalization of youth of color. Freddy's work has been published by *The Acentos Review*, *POOR Magazine*, and the University of Houston's Arte Publico Press; and most recently was featured as LoWriter of the Week selected by U.S. Poet Laureate, Juan Felipe Herrera.